10
POWERFUL LESSONS ON
HOW TO WORK WITH
CONTRACTS

HOW TO READ THEM, ENFORCE THEM AND NOT GET CHEATED.

SHAUNÈ HAWKINS LANGSTON, ESQ.
of The Langston Law Firm, PLLC

10

POWERFUL LESSONS
ON
HOW TO WORK WITH
CONTRACTS

HOW TO READ THEM,
ENFORCE THEM AND
NOT GET CHEATED

SHAUNÈ HAWKINS LANGSTON, ESQ.

http://www.langstonlawfirm.com/

10 Powerful Lessons on How to Work with Contracts: How to Read Them, Enforce Them and not Get Cheated

Shaunè Hawkins Langston, Esq.

Copyright © 2013 by Shaunè Hawkins Langston, Esq.

All Rights Reserved. No part of this book may be reproduced or distributed in any form, including but not limited to: printing, photocopying, faxing, recording, electronic transmission, or by any information storage or retrieval system without prior written permission.

All trademarks, service marks, registered trademarks, and registered service marks are the property of their respective owners and are used herein for identification purposes only.

Published by:
Shaunè Hawkins Langston, Esq.
Hawkland Media, LLC
11319 Cromwell Court
Woodbridge, VA 22192

Cover Art: Creativelog
Editor: Allie Hart
Proofreader: Novellette Whyte
Formatter and e-book conversions: Jim & Zetta, http://www.jimandzetta.com/

Notice about Piracy

Do not participate in or encourage the piracy of copyrighted materials in violation of the author's rights. Purchase only authorized editions.

TABLE OF CONTENTS

Introduction

Chapter 1: What Are Contracts?
- Implied
- Express
- Bilateral and Unilateral Contracts
- Unconscionable Contracts (Deal Breaker)
- The Wretched Handshake Deal (No Deal at All)

Chapter 2: Where Do Contracts Come into Play?
   (Um, Everywhere)

Chapter 3: How Can Contracts Affect My Life?
   The Good, the Bad, the Unnecessary and the Ugly

Chapter 4: What are Some Things to Look for in Contracts?

Chapter 5: How Do I Avoid Problems that Could Emanate From Contracts?

Chapter 6: I Have Been Cheated or I Am Being Cheated. What Should I do?

Chapter 7: What Can I do if I did not Understand Something and Made a Mistake in a Contract?

Chapter 8: Sample Contracts: On What Provisions Should You Pay Special Attention?

Chapter 9: What are Causes of Action and Remedies for Breach of Contract?

Chapter 10: Going Forward: What Should You Do When it Comes to Contracts?

About the Author

Copyrights and Trademarks Acknowledgements

INTRODUCTION

Among other things I do, for the bulk of my professional life thus far I have been an attorney. It started out with a dream. My father, the late, great James Hawkins (also known as "Hawk"), instilled in me as a young child that I was to become the next Thurgood Marshall. As a child, and not really knowing what or who a Thurgood Marshall was at the time, I agreed with him gleefully. Whenever I agreed gleefully to whatever Hawk said, it resulted in candy, piggy back rides, or a trip to the nearest 7-Eleven® convenience store so I could get a coveted big, sour pickle that I loved so much as a youth.

As I grew older and progressed through grade school, it became obvious I had a natural aptitude for reading comprehension and writing. I had a hatred and natural dislike for math and all such abstract concepts (as I considered them to be) that did not allow me room for creativity and expression. Writing was my thing. Reading was my thing. Thus, even though I went through the throes of adolescence and high school, determined to become either a nurse, a dance choreographer (á la Debbie Allen from Fame©), or a psychiatrist, by the time I got to college (intent on being an M.D., specializing in psychiatry indeed) I came to the realization that Hawk was right all along. Organic Chemistry told me loud and clear that Hawk was right all along. My talents were in reading, writing, understanding the deeper concepts under the words and regurgitating that understanding at a level of mastery that earned me Bachelor of Arts Degrees in Psychology, Political Science and a minor in Philosophy, *magna cum laude*, as well as election into the coveted fraternity of Phi Beta Kappa®. Oh yes, by the second semester of undergrad, I knew law school was where I was headed.

What I didn't know until I began the practice of law, however, was that I hated (and still hate) the adversarial process of litigation. So while Hawk almost hit the nail on the head with me being the next great Thurgood Marshall or Johnny Cochran, I turned out to be turned on in law school by courses having to do with business. Naturally, the foundation of those courses always ended up with a basis in contracts.

Sorry Hawk, Thurgood Marshall is not me, but be begrudged not; I dedicate this book to you and my Mom, Sherrie. Without you and my Great Grandmother and paternal grandparents, I would not be capable of doing all that I do today. I thank you, I miss you, and I bless your names.

So today, in my practice, The Langston Law Firm, PLLC, I specialize in transactional/business law and I love contracts like I love my right hand (and that's a lot, because I'm also an avid baton twirler, yes, even to this day at my age). It is my mission to let everyday people in on some of the mistakes, hiccups, tricks, and missteps that can take you down when you encounter a situation where you are asked to sign your name on a dotted line.

Everywhere we turn, we are inundated with contracts and the laws that rule them, but most people don't know it. The purpose of this book is to give you a tool, or a weapon in the form of knowledge to help you avoid mistakes, hiccups, tricks and missteps when it comes to your life and how contracts can affect you, yours and everything you own. And don't worry, I teach classes about contracts and business law in general—I'll do my best to make things plain and clear without the legalese everyone hates, including some lawyers themselves.

~ Shaunè H. Langston, Esq.

CHAPTER 1
WHAT ARE CONTRACTS?

At its most basic level, a contract is just another word for an agreement. A mutual understanding (a meeting of the minds) between two or more persons concerning whatever is currently being considered whereby if this happens on my part, then that happens on your part, and such understandings are enforceable. One party must make an offer and the other must accept it. That's the basis of a contract

Contracts either are, or form the underlying basis for, leases (cars, boats, apartments), mortgages, warranties, financing statements, lawyer's engagement letters and retainer agreements, parking deck agreements, divorce and child support decrees, licenses, utility service agreements, library cards, medical care, dreaded insurance policies, the admissions tickets you get to movies and theme parks, Redbox® rentals, the fare in restaurants that you eat, the understanding you have with your hairdresser, barber, baby sitter, dog walker and just about every other attribute of your life that you can think of.

As you can see, contracts are not just somewhere up in the sky with big businesses. Contracts concern all of us in almost every aspect of our lives. At the bare minimum, there's an unspoken contract we have with one another that's hardly, if ever, actually written down–that contract, or agreement, being the understanding that we treat each other in socially acceptable ways. We're not allowed to hit a person, spit on a person, trip someone on purpose, choke your boss, or any other kind of violence, and please don't yell "Fire" in a crowded movie theater. The basis for these unspoken contracts lies in the concept of public safety and common decency as we attempt to live amongst one another in peace. Violate someone; trespass on their property; try to take something from them without due payment in exchange for the taking and what happens usually? The police get involved and you likely get sued–especially if someone is hurt or property is damaged.

Contracts keep us in a uniform state of existence for the most part. If we really look at it from a distance, we've been taught the general concept of contract law since we were toddlers who could understand language.

- "Do that again, Johnny, and you'll go to your room!"
- "My grades suck. There's no way Mom and Dad will get me a car now."
- "No candy for you, Mandy. You were bad at school today. The teacher called me. GO TO YOUR ROOM!"

The basis underlying each of these examples was that if you did this, you got that. Those were give and take understandings–the same core bases of what makes up contracts. One party agrees to give someone this, and the other party agrees to give the first party that.

Similarly, if you borrow money to buy a house, you get the privilege to live in that house as long as you allow the bank you borrowed money from to put a lien on that house in the form of a mortgage. If you don't pay your mortgage, your privilege will be revoked. Similarly, if you don't pay your taxes (and you never actually get a written agreement for this usually), you'll lose your privileges to drive your vehicles (personal property taxes) and you'll lose the privilege of living in your home as it shall be sold in an auction because of unpaid property taxes.

There are several different kinds of contracts. Let's break them down, one by one. Then, if you're not already convinced, you'll really understand that your life is based upon contracts (indeed, before you are properly buried or cremated, the funeral home requires someone's payment and signature on a contract for the services) by the time you finish reading this book.

First, <u>express contracts</u> are easy to spot. These are the contracts that you knowingly enter into and that you are asked to sign off on before they are deemed fully effective or executed. You likely encounter express contracts when you rent a car, buy a house (the promissory note and the mortgage act as specialized contract types), and when you sign all that paperwork when you start a new job (those are mostly all contracts, even though some businesses may get sly and call certain forms policies; such policies are contracts–don't be tricked). Express contracts usually are between at least two people and your signature on any contract indicates that you understand and agree to every single word in that contract.

<u>Implied</u> <u>contracts</u> are usually contracts that are based on assumptions. Implied contracts are not spoken or written in words. They can take two forms. Contracts implied by fact and contracts implied by law. They are closely akin to what we expect from each other as a society. For example, when you buy a home, rent a place to live, or rent a hotel room for the night, there is usually an implied understanding that the residence or shelter is or will be habitable during your stay. If it is not, you can usually evacuate the premises and demand your money back. Moreover, in the case of implied contracts, express consent from either party is not given. The circumstances surrounding the situation that gives the presumption of an implied contract can be inferred from the relationship between the parties and the situation at hand.

Moreover, <u>contracts</u> <u>implied</u> <u>by</u> <u>law</u> are known as quasi contracts. Usually courts enforce these 'non' contracts purely to prevent one party from being unjustly enriched by the acts, services or products provided to that first party by another party. For instance, suppose your neighbor was to have his grass cut by a landscaping company tomorrow. You have this knowledge; however, when you see the landscaping company cut your grass instead of your neighbor's, when the owner of the landscaping company presents you with a bill, a court will force you to pay it based on your prior knowledge of the mistake. If you had no prior knowledge, you likely would not be liable to pay the bill – it depends on the court.

Similarly, contracts are implied between you and your local and federal government. It is implied that if you are caught by a law enforcement officer breaking a law, something as simple as running a red light or speeding, then you will likely be the recipient of a ticket that will obligate you to pay a fine for breaching the socially understood contract that you should not run red lights and you should not accelerate your vehicle beyond the speed limit at issue. It is implied that you shall pay your taxes each and every year to Uncle Sam. If you don't, you could end up in federal prison and/or with hefty fines and garnishments from your checks. The understanding or rationale here is that your tax dollars are needed to keep the country running (I think anyway—I'm not a tax attorney). But the point here is that it is implied without your express or mutual consent with Big Brother that you shall pay your taxes.

<u>Unilateral</u> <u>contracts</u> call for the performance of one of the parties in exchange for payment by the person that benefits from that first party's efforts or work. The usual scenario is where you orally agree (something I detest—I like everything in writing) to pay someone to do a service for you, such as cutting your grass, painting your house or watching your kids. It is implied that the service will be properly and effectively completed or carried out in exchange for your payment to the servicer. Unilateral contracts can be express or implied.

<u>Bilateral</u> <u>contracts</u> are simply contracts between two or more parties with the understanding that the performance or non-performance of some act is expected from one or more of the parties. These contracts can be express or implied. For example, my car breaks down. I take it to my local repair shop. They give me a complementary diagnosis of the problem

and then present me with paperwork giving them permission to do the repairs that are needed, and giving me the obligation of paying them to do so. If I fail to pay them for their work, they can place a lien on my vehicle. If they fail to properly repair my vehicle, I can sue them for breach of contract. That contract I signed could have explicitly stated every repair they would make, or it could have basically implied that the mechanic would simply repair my vehicle. Either way, the contract is bilateral as it is between two or more parties with the expectation that both will benefit from the agreement they've made.

<u>Unconscionable</u> <u>contracts</u> are contracts that go too far, in a bad way and are usually deemed void. By way of example, if you're in the market to get some home repair services from a contractor and that contractor comes out to your home, and gives you an estimate that you agree upon, all is well. But, when the contractor completes the work, and along the way has learned that his estimate was way too low for the amount of work that it would take to do the work you requested and agreed for him to do, guess what happens. He hands you a bill that is at least double or

triple the estimate. Without your consent, he took on additional expenses (if he's honest) and he performed the work—he just didn't give you the option of saying yea or nay to the increased contract price. The contractor expects you to pay the heightened price as he's already completed the work. Such a non-communication and heightened payment requirements could be arguably deemed unconscionable—meaning, not fair to the homeowner who had no clue the cost of repairs would be so much higher than the estimate she was initially given. The homeowner had no knowledge the contractor's work would cost so much and the contractor was in a superior position to the homeowner, knowledge-wise at least, to know that his bill would be considerably higher than what she expected. Many of these kinds of contractual disagreements can get you to the court house. The homeowner feels cheated and tricked, and so might the contractor who lacked the forethought to tell the homeowner that he was going way over budget on the project. You never want to find yourself in this kind of a predicament. A properly drafted contract would have a clause in it saying that if costs as estimated end up going over the estimate by a certain amount, an amendment to the contract would be necessary and the homeowner's written consent will be necessary before any additional work commenced.

The <u>oral</u> or <u>handshake</u> <u>contract</u>. Yes, in the table of contents I called such a concept wretched and that's because it is. In my practice and in your everyday life, never come to an agreement on something that is of any significance to you with a mere oral or handshake agreement. To avoid future headaches, selective memories, and a guaranteed trip to see the judge, put your contracts/agreements in writing. Like Forrest Gump©, that's all I have to say about that.

In addition to these types of contracts, there are also <u>adhesion contracts</u>, which are very similar to unconscionable contracts, but differ in one important way: adhesion contracts involve one party with superior bargaining power that gives the second party to the contract only two options, either agree to the contract or walk away from it because nothing in the contract is negotiable. Courts do not always find such contracts to be unfair. The facts of the situation must be reviewed. But for the most part, most courts won't uphold an adhesion contract because of the fact that the second party never really consented to the contract because they, in actuality, had no real choice. They had no bargaining power and courts frown upon such dealings.

Finally, contracts can be determined to be <u>void</u> or <u>voidable</u>. Usually, if a person is underage, under duress, defrauded or under the condition of some disability that effects their ability to properly reason and understand what the contract calls for them to do, the contract is void. However, if desired, when the under-aged person comes of legal age, or if the disabled party becomes able to properly reason and understand the contract, the contract can be termed "voidable" and not necessarily void. A voidable contract can come back to life and be rendered enforceable if such parties that are no longer at a disadvantage desire that result.

* * * * *

While I detest the idea of an oral contract, certain contracts MUST be in writing—a simple piece of notebook paper and a pen will suffice as long as all the terms making up the contract are present. Those include:

- Contracts regarding real property such as purchase agreements, mortgages, leases and yes, notices that you are quitting a lease (check your state law to see how far in advance such notices must be given to your landlord);
- Contracts that cannot be performed in less than a year (long term contracts);
- Contracts wherein you agree to be liable for the debt of another, such as guarantees;
- Contracts for sales over $500 or leases over $1000;
- Contracts to give property at or after a person dies;
- Contracts regarding the sale of stocks and/or bonds;
- In a few states, a contract regarding money or property in exchange for marriage (like a dowry), also known as marriage contracts.

CHAPTER 2
WHERE DO CONTRACTS COME INTO PLAY?

Contracts come into play in every arena of our lives. Living in a society such as ours, social mores, expectations, express agreements, implied understandings and unspoken rules and regulations are always hanging over our heads. As the previous chapter suggests, you can't get away from contractual obligations. By virtue of you have a driver's license and driving, you have implicitly agreed to abide by all of the rules of the road when you get behind the wheel. By virtue of you using your credit card at the gas station, you imply that you agree to pay your creditor for borrowing the money off the card to get the gas to fill up you vehicle. By virtue of you sitting in your barber's chair and allowing him to cut your hair, you implicitly agree you will pay that barber for his or her services (and maybe even tip them). Also, when you sign up to publish a book in Amazon's Kindle® or KDR Program®, guess what? You've entered a contractual relationship with Amazon®.

People put up fences around their houses for a reason. They don't take a liking to trespassers usually (at least my family didn't)—even the mailbox was on the outside of the fence with a big Pit Bull or Chow Chow running loose in the front, fenced-in yard with a *Beware of Dog* sign on it. Everyone seemed to get the message. Come in uninvited at your own risk trespasser—we wouldn't be liable. What kind of contract do you suppose we were enforcing at our family home with its fenced in, scary dog fortress? Take a guess. You're right, it was an implied contract between the Hawkins family and outsiders. If we didn't bother you or invite you to our abode, you were expected not to bother us. Only one person had to learn this the hard way, but he's since been deported....

When you pull up to a drive-through and place an order, you are in mutual agreement with the restaurant establishment that they will exchange their food for your money. That is a contract.

When you live in a townhome or condominium, where there is a community association and bylaws, they make it expressly evident that you are agreeing to abide by those bylaws in order to live in that community. That is a contract.

When you walk into a store that has had to come to the unfortunate decision to have to put up a sign saying shirts and shoes are required, if you enter that establishment, you are expected to abide by that private proprietor's rules and regulations. Walk in shirtless or shoeless and you could be made to leave. Why? Because you breached their contract, no matter how makeshift it may appear, to only enter their establishment fully clothed.

Does your pet have its rabies shots and other vaccinations? Some jurisdictions also require dog tags so if your pet is lost, its owner can be located. If such regulations are in place in your hometown, these are implied contracts that you must perform in order to be in keeping with the law.

Do you keep your children in school on a regular basis and abide by the truancy act that may be in effect in your school district? This is an example of an implied contract, whereby you are responsible for, and expected to get your child to school every day, unless they are ill.

Do you understand what I am getting at here? The law, which is really predominately based on contractual precepts, surrounds us in this country. Contracts are as ubiquitous as the air we breathe. Thus, it is important to understand contract law in order to keep yourself on the straight and narrow, and in order to be informed about your rights that some of these contracts protect and empower you with, in case you are ever cheated or victimized by another in this society.

CHAPTER 3
HOW CAN CONTRACTS AFFECT MY LIFE?

The Good

A contract or an agreement where there is mutual assent and understanding by all parties to the contract or agreement can be an awesome thing. It can enable you to move into that dream house you've always wanted; it can enable you to sign off on that loan documentation so you can pursue your educational goals; it can enable you to drive that hot Ferrari® off the lot—heck, a good contract, where all parties understand it inside and out can make your life wonderful (as long as everyone stays good and abides by the contract's terms).

The Bad

A contract that is executed, or signed, by all parties is assumed to be understood by those parties. But as I've alluded to previously, sometimes people are under duress, disabled, tricked or straight out cheated in a contract because they failed to get a clear understanding of all of the provisions and terms of the contract. This is the stuff that nightmares are made of for the parties to the contract and for the attorneys who try to mend fences, so to speak.

By way of example, say you enter an amusement park and the ticket you are given to gain admittance has all of that legal rigmarole crunched down in microscopic type on the back of it. You walk in with your twelve-year old ready to have a great time. Your twelve-year old is just barely five feet, puberty hasn't kicked in yet. Your twelve-year old desires to get on a ride that specifies that all patrons should be at least five feet, five inches, in order to safely ride the apparatus, or else injuries or even death could result. The sign that specifies this requirement and warning has been knocked down, bleached out by the sun and kicked under the bushes. You have no idea about the warning and you happily give your child the thumbs up when she asks to go stand in line and get on that ride. She's allowed on. Unfortunately though, her departure from the ride comes in an unexpected way. The bar lever is too high to hold her down and she is violently thrown from the ride. She incurs significant injuries. You, in shock, horror, and utter disbelief, immediately consult with an attorney after your daughter gets out of surgery and is deemed to be a lucky girl who will fully recover. You visit your lawyer and your lawyer asks for the amusement park ticket. You rifle through your purse, unsure if you have it, but then, there they are—two admission tickets to the amusement park.

The lawyer pulls out his magnifying glass and explains the following to you: "This ticket is evidence that you paid due consideration in the form of money in exchange for the privilege and license to enjoy the park's rides and attractions. Therefore, this is a contract or a license, which is a kind of revocable contract." He smiles. As he continues to read down further though, his smile disappears slowly.

He looks up at you somberly and comes around the desk to bend down next to you so that both of you can read the following together, with his magnifying glass: "As the purchaser of this ticket and/or guest of this theme park you hereby assume all risks and agree that this park shall be held harmless from any and all suits, demands, or claims that may result in the event that you are injured while in attendance at this park.

You fully waive all rights to come against us in any form of law suit or alternative dispute resolution in the event that you incur an injury of any kind."

The lawyer explains to you that you don't have a chance, even in heaven, to successfully sue the amusement park with this humdinger of what is called an indemnification and hold harmless clause – a common clause found in most express contracts. Your lawyer explains that he could try and argue that the clause wasn't conspicuous enough and that the park was negligent per se for not having the sign up at the ride on which your child was injured. But he admits, it would be an expensive fight and likely protracted litigation. You're his client and he leaves the decision up to you. Are you up for the fight when there is no guarantee that you could win, all based on the writing on the license/contract/admission ticket that you agreed to (even though you likely were not aware of such an indemnification and hold harmless clause) when you purchased the ticket, entered the theme park and availed yourself of all of the fun shows, treats and rides just like all the other patrons that were at the park that day?

Your lawyer tells you that if you want to go forward, he'll require at least a $15,000 retainer to do research and find out if maybe others have been injured so that he can possibly add credence to your suit with a class action, where other injured members would also be plaintiffs against the theme park. You shake your head. Fifteen thousand dollars! The lawyer shrugs his shoulders. "It is what it is dear client, and it is bad." You can't afford the gamble. Although you have been wronged, you understand that contract law has got you between a rock and a hard place. You thank your lawyer, and make your way back to the hospital, to sit with your lucky, but injured and traumatized daughter.

The Ugly

You buy what you think is your dream home, but it's actually a house of terror. In part, due to an unscrupulous seller, and a shady appraiser, you are equitably underwater as far as your house value is concerned; your home is haunted because you hear footsteps upstairs when no one else is home; and your house is infested with fleas and ticks that put your health in the direct line fire, as well as bats in the attic that are ruining your air filtration system, and pose a serious threat to your health, due to the huge amounts off guano they produce. You sank your whole life savings into buying this *dream home* that is now a nightmare. The inspector didn't point any of these issues out and the sellers' agent said nothing about it either and you can't find that darn appraiser to save your life. But you've signed off on the deal. The previous owners have given you a quitclaim deed. The house is yours, all yours and you paid for it with cash. That equals a contract. You got the deed in exchange for the money you paid to the previous owners. Granted, the contract is unfair and fraudulent, but let's read further to see if you have any options for a just outcome in this situation.

The implied warranty of habitability is surely in breach, but what do you do when the previous owners have renounced their citizenship and moved to another country in the Mediterranean? Hmmmm. This is ugly.

The previous owners and the sellers' agent sold you a deeply marred piece of real estate, and the deed you hold in your hands is indeed a kind of contract that gives you the full and total rights to full ownership of your new nightmare. You are broke. You have a job, but you were not expecting the kind of expensive remediation that it's going to take to get your new home into a livable state. The sellers' agent claims he had no idea of the problems with the property. Indeed, the sellers' agent didn't live at the property. You have no recourse–the owners are gone far and away. This is ugly.

It's so ugly that every real estate lawyer you consult turns you down for representation. It's hard to subpoena someone from outside of the country. The lawyers are sorry you have invested your life savings into a money pit, but there's nothing they can do but add to your expenses if they represent you; and there's no guarantee that they can find the previous owners and pull them back into America to hold them accountable for the fraud they pulled on you. They all inform you that if you had called them to represent you before you bit the bullet on this one, they could have checked that appraisal and compared it to other similar homes in the same zip code; suggested that you have more than one inspection since the house is a 19th century home; had an environmental consultant come in to check levels for any pollutants in the air and the water; and they would have negotiated with the sellers to give you at least a six month home warranty on the property. This is damn ugly—and all you can do is scream within the face mask you and your family have been instructed to wear until the bats can be fumigated out of the home and the deadly guano cleaned out of the attic.

Finally, contract law fails you again as you peruse the inspector's contract thoroughly and see that the inspector's contract has a hefty indemnification and hold harmless clause that you signed off on in your excitement to buy the home. All you can do is scream, because this is ugly.

CHAPTER 4
WHAT ARE SOME THINGS TO LOOK FOR IN CONTRACTS?

The following is not an exhaustive, all-inclusive list of things that you should be advocating for in your contracts, but it gives you a good start and helps to get your juices flowing when it comes to what you should want out of your contracts; depending on what side of the negotiation table you are on.

A. <u>If you are party 1 to the transaction or the seller, service provider, here's what you want in your contract:</u>
- Buyer assumes all risks.
- Waiver and Indemnification Clause (including no liability for environmental issues, if any).
- Hold Harmless Clause.
- If the buyer is a company, you want a personal, "good guy," guarantee.
- If selling a property or a tangible product, buyer accepts it in "as is" condition (also called, "as is, where is" condition).

- Buyer agrees that it has had the opportunity to inspect the subject of the contract and agrees that the subject of the contract is acceptable.
- Unless it involves the sale of real estate, a change in ownership prohibition.
- Seller's sole consent is necessary, in the case of real estate for example, for any subleasing or change in tenancy in leasing situations – seller need not give a reason for its decision. (A lease is a contract.)
- If you are signing the contract on behalf of a company, make sure you have the authority to sign on behalf of the company (usually by way of a Resolution or by way of providing such rights in your company's Bylaws (for Corporations), Operating Agreement (for LLCs), or Partnership Agreement, and use my signature block style example from Chapter 5.

B. <u>If you are party 2 to the transaction or the buyer, recipient of services, here's what you want in your contract:</u>

- A knowledge representation and warranty

statement from the seller: i.e., to the best of seller's knowledge, and based upon seller's due diligence and investigation into the subject matter of the contract, there are no issues and all is good with the subject matter of the contract.

- A representation and warranty that seller has the authority to enter into and execute the contract.
- A representation and warranty that seller is duly qualified to do business in the jurisdiction in which the contract is being enforced.
- No change in ownership prohibition if the contract is a lease of personal or real property. For example, no sale or transfer of interests in ownership (stocks in a corporation, membership interests in an LLC, or, partnership interests in a partnership) that will result in a change in who the owners of the company are, or that will result in a change in who the majority owners of a company are, shall be allowed without the express permission of the other side to the contract; and said permission is usually given at the other party's sole discretion-meaning, they don't have to give a reason if they say no to the

transfer of ownership interests being contemplated.

- Buyer has a period of time (three to six months) to walk away from the deal and obtain a refund if any representations and warranties of the Seller are found to be false.
- Seller is liable for environmental liability under all U.S. environmental laws and buyer is not liable for the same in any manner or amount.
- Seller offers a warranty if the contract involves real or personal property.
- No personal guarantees if buyer is a company.
- An accurate description of the subject(s) of the contract.
- If you are signing the contract on behalf of a company, use my signature block style example from Chapter 5.

If there are more than two parties to the contract, usually those extra parties have interests in the contract that are aligned with one of the main two parties to the contract. Those third parties should also look for the same kind of beneficial provisions as the party they are aligned with and those third parties should be sure that it is explicitly provided that those beneficial provisions apply to said third parties as well. Special provisions may need to be inserted for third parties to the contract—particularly provisions that clearly render them as not being liable in any way should any problems occur under the contract (unless, of course, their own negligence or intentional acts causes any such possible problems under the contract). Third parties to contracts have rights too. If a party breaches a contract and that breach negatively effects the benefit that the third party expected from the contract, that breaching party may also be found liable to the third party for damages.

CHAPTER 5
HOW DO I PREVENT PROBLEMS THAT COULD EMANATE FROM CONTRACTS?

Yes, I'm going to say it, consult an attorney and let the specialized knowledge and craft they have studied and practiced for years do the leg work for you. If the lawyer is worth their flesh, they'll bring up special provisions and considerations that you should be aware of.

Understandably, everyone cannot afford a good lawyer. As such, my next piece of advice is simple. Make sure you read, read, read, and re-read the contract and understand, understand, understand and have complete understanding of the contract before you sign your name on the dotted line for anything. Be careful.

If you are signing off on a contract as a business, sign as the business with your signature underneath the business' name and your title in the business. For example, study the following signature block:

Buyer: The Money House, LLC

10 Powerful Lessons On How To Work With Contracts

By: Barbara Hoffheimer

Signature:_____

Title: Managing Member

I have a horror story from Hades that involved the mistake a client made while signing off on a contract. It ended up making her personally liable when the case went to court. It was a nightmare.

It is a lawyer's job to dot every 'i' and to cross every 't' BEFORE you sign your name to anything. That way you likely will avoid litigation when everything stops coming up roses in the deal. Little things mean a lot when it comes to contracts. Therefore, I can't emphasize it enough, raise money if you have to, but at least take in one good session with a lawyer and equip yourself as best as you can before executing a contract.

Nothing can replace a good lawyer. Not law in a box items, not your cousin who had two semesters of law school before he dropped out, not your business partners, not free documents online, not documents you pay for online, and not you by yourself. It may be pricey at the outset of your deal to consult with a good, experienced lawyer, but when things feel like they are starting to go sour, you'll likely kiss yourself in the mirror for having put the insurance policy of a good lawyer in place at the beginning of the deal.

Moreover, a good lawyer can alert you to things you are unaware of about the law. You may be signing off on an agreement that may put you in the hole, all because you didn't understand the consequences of what you were signing. I admit it, the law is tricky, and that is exactly why you need an expert to review your agreements before you execute them. This money on the front end usually saves clients a lot of heartburn and empty pockets on the back end when you end up burned and in court without a leg to stand on.

And believe it or not, some of us truly are in this business to help people, and money is not the primary motivating force of our practices.

CHAPTER 6
I HAVE BEEN CHEATED OR I AM BEING CHEATED. WHAT SHOULD I DO?

First, confer with the other party(ies) to the contract and see if you can meet and rectify the situation or come to some understanding that will set things right for you as intended. If this does not work, I'm going to say it again, call a good, experienced lawyer who is adept at the issues that can come up in contract law.

If someone is blatantly in breach of contract and you are the victim, you can sue that party yourself. The reasonable approach is to give them time to cure the problem. The contract should have such a cure and notice provision in it (a provision that allows the other side to notify you of a breach or some shortcoming on your part under the contract and that gives you a certain amount of time to 'cure' that breach or shortcoming before further legal actions are pursued). So you keep following the contract in letting them know that you've noticed a discrepancy and that you expect it to be remedied to completion as prescribed by the contract. If at the end of that prescribed cure period the breach continues, contact a lawyer and let them take over. Sometimes a letter from a lawyer's office is all you need to set things right. Court can be rendered unnecessary once the other side knows that you mean business. When you bring your lawyer into the mix, the other side gets the warning and knows that you are not backing down.

Short of court, there are also other avenues you can take to try to steer a contract back in the right direction. If the contract provides for the option, and even if it doesn't, you can suggest mediation or arbitration to the other side in lieu of a court proceeding. Be careful though. Dependent upon your jurisdiction and the way your contract reads, if you engage in these alternative dispute methods such as mediation or arbitration, the decisions handed down in such proceedings can be binding and foreclose you from any further opportunity to pursue the matter before an actual judge.

Do not rest on your laurels though. If you advise the other side that you are aware that you are being cheated and they don't make a move in the direction of correction, then you need to become more proactive and start making big, bold moves. A lawyer's letter to the other side's office usually does the trick. But if not, again, there's always the court room or mediation/arbitration. But move quick and move strong. Contract law, heck the law itself, rewards the proactive and the swift. If you're being cheated or the contract is being breached take action NOW! Fight for your rights. Business is business, it's not about worrying if other people will like you.

CHAPTER 7
WHAT CAN I DO IF I DID NOT UNDERSTAND SOMETHING AND MADE A MISTAKE IN A CONTRACT?

The great thing about contract law is this: A contract can always be amended. In this same vein of thought, it is prudent for you to remain civil and to try to maintain a good working relationship with the other side to the contract. If your relationships are not strained, obviously the other side will be more likely to work with you and correct whatever mistake or misunderstanding you realize you now have. If relationships are strained though, whether you get a lawyer or not, that makes it hard for mistakes to be amicably fixed and a lot of egos will be having a field day at your expense.

In this latter case where there has been a mistake and relationships between you and the other party to the contract are not good, note that the law provides that if there was no mutual understanding, and a mistake renders the contract into something different than what was intended by both parties, and the other party has been going along just dandy even though you have made a mistake and they know about it, but don't complain, then the contract can be voided. Mutual mistake can void a contract.

However, the other side of the coin is that if the mistake is purely of your own doing, and your failure to read through, do your due diligence, ask questions and truly understand what you were signing before you signed it, the shoe may drop on your head and the other party to the contract can claim you are in breach if you fail to keep performing under the contract as usual.

As is the case in all legal matters, the facts of the particular situation are what reveal the options that may be available to you. If you are nervous about bringing up the issue with the other side, consult an attorney. Situations such as this, again, are why attorneys should be retained from the beginning. Attorneys are your advocates and they hold your relationship with them in confidence. So if there was something you did not understand from the beginning, an attorney could have made it plain for you or redrafted the section all together and negotiated on your behalf to make the contract work better for you. When you bring in an attorney post mortem, that attorney's job is hard as all hell to try to help you fix the damage or the breach that has already occurred. More time is usually needed and therefore more money is usually required.

But a good attorney will give you all he or she has got to get things back on the right track as far as the contract is concerned. In many circumstances I have experienced, positive outcomes have occurred in situations where my client has breached or made a mistake under a contract. Usually, once you get a hold of the other side's attorney, and unsurprisingly, the other side usually does have their own attorneys, reasonable and cool heads usually prevail and an amendment or an addendum to the agreement can usually be worked out and the transaction can reset on the right track from that point on out.

Be warned here: if you know you have breached a contract or have made a mistake, contact your attorney or if you have a good working relationship with the other side, and your gut feels comfortable enough to contact the other side directly, then do so. But at the end of the day lawyers will need to be consulted and involved to amend the contract, add an addendum, or work out the situation in a fair and equitable way for all parties to the contract.

CHAPTER 8
SAMPLE CONTRACTS: ON WHAT PROVISIONS SHOULD YOU PAY SPECIAL ATTENTION?

This chapter will review a couple of sample contracts. Additionally, the chapter will cover provisions that should be given special attention. What follows is a sample management and leasing agreement. It is not representative of the vast universe of contracts. But I want to show you a thorough contract and where you see bracketed notes next to certain provisions (which will be underlined) see my comments (which will be bold) about the importance of such a provision. Please think on and perhaps apply my suggestions to contracts you are currently considering, or contact an attorney to help you make your contract as complete, accurate and airtight as possible.

* * * * *

THIS MANAGEMENT AND LEASING AGREEMENT (<u>Agreement</u>) is made and entered into as of the *[ordinal number of day]* day of *[name of month]*,*[designation of year]* by and between *[name of owner]*(Owner) and *[name of agent]* (Agent). **[GIVE THE FULL AND ACCURATE NAMES OF THE PARTIES TO THE CONTRACT. IF YOU MESS UP HERE, SOMEONE COULD END UP BEING PERSONALLY LIABLE. THE SAME GOES FOR THE SIGNATURE BLOCKS AT THE END OF CONTRACTS AS DISCUSSED ABOVE IN CHAPTER 5]**

WITNESSETH:

WHEREAS, Owner owns a certain tract of land located in

[Address of land],

on which exists a shopping center known as

[Name of shopping center]

Center, such tract of land and the shopping center being more particularly described on Exhibit A, attached hereto and incorporated herein by reference (which land and shopping center are hereinafter collectively referred to as the Project); and **[IF YOUR CONTRACT HAS ANYTHING TO DO WITH REAL ESTATE, WHETHER IT BE A HOME, A SPOT IN A STRIP MALL, A CONDO, STORE, OR EVEN A PARKING SPACE, MAKE SURE THE LEGAL DESCRIPTION OF THAT PIECE OF PROPERTY IS THOROUGHLY SPELLED OUT AND DEFINED. USUALLY A METES AND BOUNDS DESCRIPTION AND A RENDERING OF THE REAL PROPERTY ARE INCLUDED AS EXHIBITS (ADD ONS AT THE END) TO THE CONTRACT]**

WHEREAS, Owner desires to employ Agent to manage and lease the Project subject to the terms of this Agreement; and

NOW, THEREFORE, in consideration of the mutual covenants and conditions contained herein, and other good and valuable considerations, receipt and sufficiency of which are hereby acknowledged, Owner and Agent, intending to be legally bound, hereby agree as follows **[SEE THE MUTUALITY OF ASSENT, AGREEMENT AND UNDERSTANDING HERE – THESE ARE THE COMPONENTS OF A VALID CONTRACT; BOTH PARTIES ARE ON THE SAME PAGE]**:

1. *Employment and Appointment.*
Owner hereby employs Agent for the term of this Agreement as its sole and exclusive manager and leasing Agent of the Project. Owner further appoints and designates Agent as its duly authorized representative to perform the functions and services listed herein in the name of and on behalf of Owner, all at Owner's sole cost and expense. Agent hereby accepts such employment and appointment on the terms and conditions set forth herein.

2. *Term.*
Owner hereby employs Agent to manage, lease, re-lease, and maintain the Project for a term of one (1) year from the date hereof, automatically renewable annually unless sooner terminated **[ANOTHER VERY IMPORTANT PART OF A CONTRACT IS THE TERM – HOW LONG WILL IT LAST**

AND WHEN WILL IT EXPIRE? MAKE SURE THIS IS CLEARLY UNDERSTOOD BY BOTH PARTIES]** pursuant to the provisions of paragraph 8 hereof.

3. *Functions and Services of Agent*. **[DUTIES: IT IS ESPECIALLY IMPORTANT TO SPELL OUT EXACTLY WHAT IS TO BE EXPECTED FROM EACH OF THE PARTIES TO A CONTRACT]**
Agent agrees to perform, and shall have full power and authority for, on behalf of, and in the name of Owner, the following services as manager and leasing agent of the Project, and Agent shall have authority to expend such sums and incur such expenditures (subject to the terms of this Agreement), all at Owner's expense, as may be necessary in connection therewith:

(a) Investigate, hire, pay, supervise, and discharge the personnel necessary to be employed in order to properly maintain and operate the Project, including janitor and maintenance personnel.

(b) Advertise the Project in such manner as deemed

advisable by Agent and Owner;

(c) Investigate prospective tenants, rent space in the Project to tenants on such terms and conditions as may be specified by Owner, and, in accordance with the terms and conditions of a <u>Purchase Agreement</u> dated the
[Ordinal number of day]

day of
[Name of month],

[Designation of year]

<u>executed between these parties and incorporated herein by reference</u>. **[WHEN REFERENCING OTHER DOCUMENTS TO BE INCLUDED IN THE PRESENT CONTRACT, THIS IS THE WAY TO DO IT - "INCORPORATED HEREIN BY REFERENCE." BE SURE YOU UNDERSTAND THAT ADDITIONAL PART OF THE CONTRACT TOO!]**

(d) Collect, demand, request, and receive rentals, percentage rentals, common area maintenance charges, payments toward taxes and insurance, security deposits, and such other sums which may be due from tenants;

(e) Terminate tenancies and refund tenant security deposits where deemed advisable by Owner; sign and serve such notices as are deemed needed by Owner or Agent; institute and prosecute actions to cost tenants and to recover possession of tenant space in the Project; sue and recover rent;

(f) Cause the buildings, appurtenances, and grounds of the Project to be maintained and kept in repair, as may be deemed necessary by Owner to keep the Project in first class operation;

(g) Take such action as may be necessary to comply with any and all orders or requirements affecting the Project which shall be issued or imposed by any federal, state, county, or municipal authority having jurisdiction thereof; provided, however, that Agent shall promptly notify Owner in writing of all such orders and notices or requirements and comply with Owner's instructions regarding such orders and requirements, to the extent that such instruction can practically and legally be followed;

(h) Make contracts and arrangements for securing water, electricity, gas, fuel, oil, and other services necessary for the successful operation of the Project;

(i) If requested by Owner, obtain and keep in full force and effect, at Owner's expense, all insurance which may be specified in writing by Owner. Unless specified in writing by Owner, Agent shall have the right to determine companies, amounts of coverage, and forms of policies, including riders and endorsements, as shall be deemed necessary by Agent, provided that Agent shall not be held liable to Owner in respect of any such determination which is made in good faith. Agent may have itself designated as an additional insured under any of the policies;

(j) From funds collected and deposited in the account hereinafter provided, cause to be disbursed regularly and punctually: (i) salaries and any other compensation due and payable to the employees of Owner; (ii) the single aggregate payment required to be made monthly to any lender, including the amount due under each mortgage note, if any, for premium charges under the contract of insurance, taxes and assessments, fire and other hazard insurance premiums, interest on each mortgage loan; and (iii) sums otherwise due and payable by Owner as operating expenses which are incurred pursuant to the terms of this Agreement including management and other fees as provided herein;

(k) Cooperate with Owner's accountants in preparation for execution and filing by Owner of all forms, reports, and returns required by law in connection with unemployment insurance, workers' compensation insurance, disability benefits, and social security not in effect or hereafter imposed, and also all requirements relating to the employment of personnel;

(l) Agent agrees that, within fifteen (15) days after the execution hereof, it will prepare and submit to Owner for its approval a budget setting forth the estimated receipts and expenditures (capital, operating, and other) of the Project for the balance of the current calendar year. When a budget (including any revision thereof and a budget for calendar years *[designation of calendar years]*) submitted by Agent has been approved by Owner in writing, Agent shall be authorized to make the expenditures and incur the obligations provided for in said budget. Agent shall not be authorized to incur any obligations or to make any expenditures for or on behalf of the Owner not set forth in an approved budget unless such obligation or expenditure is approved in advance in writing by the Owner. Notwithstanding the foregoing, Agent shall have the right, without further approval of the Owner, to make an expenditure or incur an obligation not set forth in an approved budget provided that: (i) such obligation or expenditure does not involve a sum in excess of $ _____

[Dollar amount of sum],

and (ii) such expenditure or obligation when added to all other expenditures or obligations, made or to be made, or incurred or to be incurred, by Agent on behalf of Owner in such year which have not been otherwise approved in writing does not or will not cause the aggregate amount of all such expenditures and obligations to exceed the approved budget for such year by more than $_____.

[Dollar amount of excess]

(2) Additionally, in the event the Agent, in its good faith and reasonable judgment, deems an expenditure not provided for in an approved budget to be an emergency
(that is immediately necessary to protect persons or property).

(3) Agent shall be authorized to make such expenditure on behalf of the Owner, provided that Agent notifies Owner by telephone of the nature of the emergency and the scope of the work to be done, and immediately confirms the same in writing, which confirmation shall include evidence as to all costs incurred to date and Agent's best estimate of the total cost thereof.

(m) Agent agrees to keep full and detailed books and records covering the management of the Project and to provide reasonable accounting services with respect to the project and submit to the Owner the following unaudited statements at the time hereinafter specified: (i) within ten (10) days from the end of each month, a statement showing the gross sales reports of each tenant received to date; (ii) within ten (10) days from the end of each month, detailed statements consisting of a balance sheet, cash flow statement, income statements, statement of receipts and disbursements, receivables, and, if available, payables.

Owner shall at all times have access to such records as well as to the other books and records of the Agent maintained on behalf of the Owner and directly related to the leasing, operation, maintenance, and management of the Project, and the Owner's accountants shall have the right to audit such books and records.

Agent shall not be responsible for preparing or filing any audited financial statements or tax, corporate, or other related returns or forms, but agrees, if requested by Owner, to make available records which may be necessary for the Owner's accountants to prepare and file such reports. Notwithstanding the foregoing, Agent will be responsible for filing payroll tax returns for Owner's employees working at the Project;

(n) Select, contract, supervise the performance of, and pay the fees and charges for, all independent contractors required for proper maintenance and operation of the Project;

(o) If requested by Owner, Agent would agree to appeal before any taxing authorities any property tax assessments relative to the Project.

4. *Bank Account.*
Agent shall establish and maintain, in a bank whose deposits are insured by the Federal Deposit Insurance Corporation and in a manner to indicate the custodial nature thereof, a separate bank account as Agent of the Owner, or, at the option of the Owner, a bank account in the name of the Owner or of the Project, for the deposit of monies of the Owner. Agent shall have authority to endorse checks

payable to Owner, deposit funds of Owner into the account, and to draw on such account or accounts any payment to be made by Agent to discharge any of the liabilities or obligations incurred by Agent pursuant to this Agreement, and be subject to the limitations set forth in this Agreement.

5. *Compensation to Agent; Payments to and Reimbursement of Agent.*

(a) Compensation to Agent. In consideration of the management and leasing functions to be performed by Agent under this Agreement, Owner shall compensate Agent as follows:

(i) Management fees equal to 3% of gross income (determined on the cash method of accounting) on all base rent, common area maintenance charges, and percentage rent received from tenants in the Project.

(ii) A leasing fee equal to one (1) month's rent for all new leases (that is, a lease not identified on the Rent Roll as defined in the Purchase Agreement) having a term of more than one (1) year. This provision is not intended to be applicable to any renewal of any existing lease in the Project or any sublease under the Master Lease (as defined in the Purchase Agreement).

(iii) Anything to the contrary notwithstanding, in the event that, at the expiration date of this Agreement, there are payments due Owner pursuant to tenant leases, but which are then uncollected, and any such amount subsequently is collected, Owner shall pay Agent at the time of collection the amount Agent would have been entitled to pursuant to the terms of this Agreement had the tenant performed at the time and as required under its lease.

(b) *Payment to and Reimbursement of Agent.*
Upon the prior approval of Owner, Agent may disburse to itself upon receipt of the gross monthly payments due Owner from tenant, all amounts due Agent pursuant to this Agreement from the account or accounts maintained in accordance with the terms hereof. If the funds in such accounts are insufficient to pay Agent all amounts due it hereunder, Owner

agrees to pay Agent such amounts due Agent promptly upon Agent's request therefor. In the event Agent should advance any amount from its own funds, rather than from the funds of Owner, in the payment of any of the costs or expenses of Owner, Owner shall promptly reimburse Agent at Agent's request, or Agent may reimburse itself from the account or accounts maintained in accordance with the provisions hereof. Nothing herein contained shall be deemed or construed to require Agent to advance its own funds on behalf of Owner.

6. *Insurance.*

Owner agrees to carry public liability insurance, workers' compensation insurance, and such other insurance as may be necessary for protection of both the interests of Owner and Agent. In each such policy of Insurance, Owner agrees upon request by Agent to designate Agent as a party insured with Owner. The carrier shall be licensed in the State of

[Name of state]

and may be selected by Owner. The amount of coverage of such policies shall be mutually agreed upon by Owner and Agent. A certificate of each policy issued by the carrier shall be delivered to Agent by Owner.

7. *Indemnification and Other Agreements.*

(a) Everything done by Agent pursuant to the provisions of this Agreement shall be done as agent of the Owner, and all obligations incurred hereunder, except as specified otherwise, shall be for the account of, at the expense of, and on behalf of, the Owner, except that Owner shall not be obligated to pay any overhead expenses of Agent;

(b) <u>Owner agrees to indemnify, defend, and hold harmless Agent from and against any and all claims, actions, damages, loss, liabilities, and expenses, including, without limitation, attorney's fees, accounting fees, and court costs which Agent may incur or which may arise out of or on account of this Agreement and the performance of the duties and services set forth herein and from liability for personal injury, including death, or property damage experienced by any employee or other person or</u>

entity whatsoever; provided, however, that this section shall not impose any obligation on Owner to indemnify Agent against the willful misconduct or gross negligence of Agent; **[A GOOD EXAMPLE OF AN INDEMNIFICATION AND HOLD HARMLESS PROVISION]**

(c) Agent does not assume and is given no responsibility for compliance of the Project or any equipment therein with the requirements of any statute, ordinance, law, or regulation of any governmental body or of any public authority or official thereof having jurisdiction, except to notify the Owner promptly or forward to the Owner promptly any complaints, warnings, notices, or summonses received by it relating to such matters. **[THIS REPRESENTS AN EXAMPLE OF AN OUT CLAUSE FOR THE AGENT]**

8. *Early Termination.* **[DEFINE EXACTLY HOW YOU OR THE OTHER PARTY CAN GET OUT OF THE CONTRACT; UNDER WHAT CONDITIONS WILL A TERMINATION OCCUR. SPELL IT OUT THOROUGHLY]**

Notwithstanding anything in this Agreement to the contrary, Owner shall have the right to terminate the Agreement as of the end of any calendar month upon the giving of thirty (30) days' notice to the other party in advance of such termination date. No liability shall attach to either party by reason of such termination provided, however, that to the extent either party has liabilities or obligations to the other existing as of the date of such termination, such liabilities or obligations shall be met and satisfied notwithstanding such termination.

Upon termination of this Agreement for any reason, the Agent shall promptly deliver the following to the Owner or the Owner's appointed agent:

(a) A final accounting for the Project, reflecting the balance of income and expenses for the Project as of the date of termination;

(b) Any balance of monies due to the Project or tenant security deposits, or both, held by the Agent with respect to the Project; and

(c) All written data and materials belonging to the Project, including all records, contracts, leases, receipts for deposits, unpaid bills, a summary of all leases in existence at the time of termination, and all other papers, plans, books, drawings, documents, and writings which pertain to the Project or the business or affairs of the Project. Such data and information and all such documents shall at all times be the property of the Project.

9. *Indemnification by Agent.*
<u>The Agent hereby absolutely, unconditionally, and irrevocably covenants and agrees to indemnify and hold harmless</u>
<u>*[Name of owner]*</u>

<u>from and against any and all claims, demands, liabilities, losses, costs, or expenses arising out of or in any way connected with any acts, omissions to act, or forbearances of the Agent, its agents, employees, or representatives, which are in violation of the duties of the Agent set forth in this Agreement or which are negligent.</u> **[ANOTHER WAY TO INDEMNIFY AND HOLD HARMLESS]**

10. Relationship of Parties.

This Agreement shall not be construed as creating a partnership agreement between the parties.

11. Modification.

<u>No change or modification of this Agreement shall be valid or binding upon the parties hereto, nor shall any waiver of any terms or condition in the future, unless such change, modification, or waiver shall be in writing and signed by the parties.</u> **[IMPORTANT, STATE IT PLAIN AND CLEAR THAT ALL AMENDMENTS, ADDENDA, CHANGES AND MODIFICATIONS ARE TOO MADE IN WRITING AND ATTACHED TO THE ORIGINAL DOCUMENT. THIS KEEPS THE CURRENT STATUS OF THE CONTRACT STREAMLINED AND CONSISTENT AS BETWEEN THE PARTIES AND THEIR UNDERSTANDING OF THE CONTRACT]**

12. Binding Effect.

This Agreement shall inure to the benefit of and be binding upon the parties hereto, their legal representatives, transferees, successors, and assigns.

[IT MAY LOOK INNOCUOUS, BUT THIS PROVISION IS A BIG DEAL. THE CONTRACT LIVES ON, EVEN IF YOU DON'T; SO MAKE SURE THE CONTRACT SAYS WHAT YOU WANT IT TO SAY]

13. *Duplicate Originals.*

For the convenience of the parties hereto, any number of counterparts hereof may be executed, and each counterpart shall be deemed to be an original.

14. *Notices.*

All notices, requests, and communications required or permitted hereunder shall be in writing and shall be sufficiently given and deemed to have been received upon personal delivery or, if mailed, upon the first to occur of actual receipt or forty-eight (48) hours after being placed in the United States mail, postage prepaid, registered or certified mail, return receipt requested. Until changed in writing by either party to this Agreement, each party's address is as follows:

(a) If to Owner:

[Name of owner],

[Address of owner]

(b) If to Agent:

[Name of agent],

[Address of agent]

15. *Entire Agreement*.

This Agreement is intended by the parties hereto to be the final expression of their Agreement and is a complete and exclusive statement of the terms thereof. **[THE DOCTRINE OF MERGER: ANY PRIOR UNDERSTANDINGS, TERM SHEETS, MEMORANDUMS OF UNDERSTANDING, LETTERS OF INTENT, ETC., NO LONGER ARE VIABLE. THIS CONTRACT IS THE FINAL AND ULTIMATE EXPRESSION OF WHAT THE PARTIES ARE AGREEING TO. SO MAKE SURE EVERYTHING YOU WANT IN THE CONTRACT IS IN IT BEFORE YOU SIGN OFF ON IT]**

IN WITNESS WHEREOF, the parties have hereunto set their hands and seals this
[Ordinal number of day]

day of
[Name of month],

[Designation of year].

_____ *[Name of owner]*

_____ *[Name of agent]* **[THESE ARE NOT GOOD SIGNATURE BLOCKS IF THE PARTIES TO THE CONTRACT ARE INDIVIDUALS THAT ARE SIGNING ON BEHALF OF A COMPANY. REVIEW MY SAMPLE SIGNATURE BLOCK IN CHAPTER 5]**

* * * * *

Below is an example of another contract that I drafted from scratch. It was something novel that I had to create from the ethers based on the unusual business deal a client wanted to pursue. The client did not want to enter into a partnership, joint venture, contractor nor other normal, par for the course type of relationship with Party 2 to the contract. That's what made the contract/agreement hard to define, and the terms of the contract/agreement difficult to produce.

With that said, however, notice the specificity and the various beneficial clauses within the contract that I installed intentionally to protect the client who was party 1 to the contract, but that also worked out to benefit both parties equally for the most part. Sometimes, indeed, most times, it is best to be square with both parties to a contract and not give the perception of overt one-sidedness. Such perceptions of inequality or unfairness can kill deals before the basic terms of the contract/agreement are even fully fleshed out in spoken word. Because this contract was so novel, and the parties hardly knew each other, the concept of fairness between the two parties was tantamount.

An experienced attorney should be able to be creative enough to come up with a contract that gets the job done, no matter how new the ideas underlying the contract are. Allow this example to also get you juices flowing when it comes to ideas and concepts that may benefit you in your contractual transactions. It is short, pithy and to the point.

*****

ALLIANCE AGREEMENT

THIS ALLIANCE AGREEMENT (alternatively referred to hereinafter as the "<u>Agreement</u>") is made to be effective as of the <u>6</u>th day of February, 2012, by and between:

Party 1, a Virginia limited liability company, represented herein by its CEO and Founder, _____ (hereinafter referred to as "<u>Party 1</u>"); and Party 2, a North Carolina limited liability company, represented herein by its CEO, _____ (hereinafter referred to as "<u>Party 2</u>") (each of Party 1 or Party 2 being sometimes herein referred to individually as a "Party" or collectively as the "Parties") for the purposes, causes and considerations enumerated hereinafter.

WITNESSETH, that

WHEREAS, both Party 1 and Party 2 are currently active in furnishing their respective services to the entertainment industry; and WHEREAS, both PARTY 1 and PARTY 2 recognize that their respective strengths and capabilities relative to the entertainment industry are complementary and supportive of, and not in competition with, each other and that an alliance of their efforts in pursuing the entertainment market for the limited and sole purpose of placing certain artists and athletes in venues in Charlotte, North Carolina for the 100th CIAA Tournament® Event Weekend offers mutual advantages and economies of scale; and

WHEREAS, PARTY 1 and PARTY 2 have agreed that it is in their mutual best interests to enter into a strategic alliance (the "Alliance"), to maximize their respective capabilities and business potential in providing high quality services the entertainment industry, combining their respective strengths, connections, relationships, market presence and expertise; and,

WHEREAS, PARTY 1 and PARTY 2's specific obligations and understanding under this Agreement are further defined in Exhibit A, the Alliance Agreement Specific Terms by and between Party 1 and Party 2, hereby incorporated herein, made a part hereof and attached hereto.

NOW, THEREFORE, the Parties hereto, acting through their duly authorized representatives, have agreed to form and administer the Alliance pursuant to the terms and conditions contained herein.

I: <u>SCOPE</u>

1.1 Subject only to any specific exceptions which may be contained in this Agreement, the Alliance shall be an exclusive alliance between PARTY 1 and PARTY 2, for the limited and sole purpose of placing certain artists and athletes in venues in Charlotte, North Carolina for the 100th CIAA Tournament® Event Weekend (the "<u>Booking Event</u>"). The exclusivity provided for herein shall apply to all services related to the Booking Event, whether such opportunities or services are generated by PARTY 1 or PARTY 2.

The use of the term 'Alliance' in describing activities to be conducted by the Parties pursuant to this Agreement, shall be construed to mean only activities to be conducted jointly by the Parties for their mutual benefit. As more fully set forth in Section 2.4 hereof, the 'Alliance' is not a separate entity but is merely intended to be a descriptive term to refer to the Parties when conducting combined operations under this Agreement.

1.2 It is recognized by the Parties that an exclusive Alliance will require that both PARTY 1 and PARTY 2 develop and cultivate a good faith course of dealing and a teamwork relationship which is based on common objectives, mutual respect and a high degree of trust. In that regard, the Parties covenant and agree that, in considering one's own best interests in any given situation related to the Alliance, the best interests of the Alliance as a whole shall also be taken into account.

1.3 To the extent that either Party is unable, or unwilling, to give full support to the efforts of the Alliance in a given instance, such Party shall notify the other Party of any such constraints and the Parties agree to work to minimize the effect of such constraints on the Alliance. It is the stated intent of both PARTY 1 and PARTY 2, in executing this Agreement, to put forth their respective best efforts to make the Alliance work for their mutual benefit and it is recognized that only through cooperation and the full and unfettered exchange of information can the mutual operations be conducted most effectively.

1.4 In the event either Party is unable, or fails for any reason, to provide its services to which the Alliance has been committed, the other Party may align itself with any other party or entity to perform the contracted services without throwing this Agreement into default; provided that prior to taking any such action, the Parties shall utilize their best efforts to attempt to resolve any problem which may be effecting the Party which is temporarily unable to perform. In the event of more than three (3) occurrences of such problems, which materially affects the performance of the Alliance, the Parties may agree to an early termination of this Agreement.

Furthermore, cause for termination shall be limited (i) to a fundamental breach by one of the Parties hereto of the provisions of this Agreement; (ii) to a change in business circumstances of either of the Parties; (iii) to a failure of the Alliance to generate economically viable business; or (iv) to the failure of either Party to engage in good faith dealing hereunder.

1.5 Each Party is responsible for the performance and quality of its own respective services as furnished to the common goals of the Alliance.

1.6 Nothing contained herein shall be construed to prohibit either Party from continuing to provide services to the marketplace, either alone or in concert with others, so long as such activities do not concern and are in no way related to the Booking Event.

II: RELATIONS BETWEEN THE PARTIES

2.1 In conducting operations pursuant to the Alliance, it is anticipated that PARTY 1 will, normally, act as the primary marketer and lead connection to the Artists and Athletes that may make an appearance or perform in the local venues for the Booking Event. PARTY 1 shall also be responsible for facilitating the initial receipt and disbursement of Booking Appearance fees to be received from the Vendors/Owners of the interested venues. PARTY 2 will act as the local contact and primary communicator to the local venues where the Athletes and Artists may be retained for performances and appearances.

2.2 Notwithstanding the provisions of the immediately preceding clause, the Parties agree that, regardless of which Party is the lead point of contact for a given performance or appearance, in the provision of services pursuant to the Alliance, as contemplated by this Agreement, such services shall only be marketed and furnished subject to the terms of this Agreement, which incorporates the specific terms of the booking selections letter dated as of January 29, 2012 from Party 1 to prospective Vendors and Owners, unless the Parties mutually agree otherwise.

2.3 In the event the Artist/Athlete or Vendor/Owner insists on the right to deal exclusively with either PARTY 2 or PARTY 1 separately, each Party may agree to a separate Contract with such Artist/Athlete or Vendor/Owner, but the Parties shall continue to work together under this Agreement as if only one Contract were in place, in order to maintain the maximum operational efficiency of the Alliance.

2.4 Notwithstanding any provision hereof which may indicate otherwise, it is the specific intent of the Parties that this Agreement and the Alliance created hereby is to be construed only as a business alliance between two independent business entities and is not, nor shall it be deemed to be, a separate entity, joint venture, or a partnership or any similar arrangement, nor shall any master/servant or employer/employee relationship be created between the Parties. Each Party hereto is an independent contractor and each Party shall control the methods and means by which its own services are provided through the Alliance, pursuant to this Agreement.

2.5 Each Party hereto shall remain responsible for the payment of its own taxes and, by executing this Agreement, neither Party shall be deemed to accept any responsibility for the payment of any taxes accruing to the other Party, whether under this Agreement or otherwise, and each Party shall release, protect, defend, indemnify and hold the other Party harmless in that regard.

2.6 The employees of PARTY 1 shall not be

deemed to be the employees, servants or agents of PARTY 2, nor shall the employees of PARTY 2 be deemed to be the employees, servants or agents of PARTY 1. Each Party shall be, and shall remain, fully responsible for its own employees and for any contract or seconded personnel furnished by it for tasks including, but not limited to, the payment of all salaries, wages, bonuses and all employment related taxes, benefits, insurance and medical costs and each Party agrees to release, protect, defend, indemnify and hold the other Party harmless in that regard.

2.7 Neither Party shall be responsible or liable to the other Party for any direct, indirect, punitive or consequential damage, including, without limitation, those related to loss of profits, loss of production, loss of business or business opportunity or similar losses, and each Party agrees to release, indemnify and hold the other harmless in that regard.

2.8 It is recognized that, in dealings with third party Vendors and Owners of clubs and venues and/or with Athletes and Artists, the ability to negotiate favorable terms is not always available. However, initial terms regarding Appearance Fees, Hotel and Travel Accommodations have been discussed and provided per the initial booking selections letter to Vendors and Owners dated as of January 29, 2012. As such, it is an integral part of this Alliance Agreement that neither Party hereto may commit the other Party to any contract terms or conditions that are in any way contrary to the initial booking selections letter described above, without the express written agreement of such other Party thereto.

2.9 As between the Parties, the provisions of this Agreement shall govern all relations between them, but such provisions shall not confer any rights unto any person or entity who is not a Party hereto.

2.10 In their relations with third parties, including Vendors, Owners, Athletes, Artists and other such parties pursuant to the Alliance, the Parties recognize that there will always be the possibility of having conflicts develop between their respective interests. Each Party covenants with the other to not knowingly commit any act which might jeopardize the rights of the other Party hereto. Each Party agrees to avoid any impropriety in dealing with third parties which might reflect adversely on the other Party or on the Alliance.

2.11 The Parties agree that neither of them will give, grant or furnish to any party, whether a customer or not, any gift, gratuity, bribe or other inducement or illegal payment which might adversely affect the operations of the Parties jointly under the Alliance, or which would otherwise be contrary to law.

III: GENERAL

3.1 In relation to the rights and obligations of each Party hereunder, it is specifically the intent of the Parties that all indemnities given hereunder shall include the indemnitee's parent, subsidiary and affiliated companies or entities, and the directors, officers, employees, servants and agents of any of them.

3.2 Except to the extent inconsistent with, or in conflict with, any U.S. laws, both Parties agree that they will comply with and abide by all laws, rules and regulations, whether governmental, legal or contractual and that, in conducting operations pursuant to the Alliance, each Party shall be, and shall remain, fully responsible for its own compliance with such laws, rules and regulations. Each Party agrees to release, protect, defend, indemnify and hold the other Party harmless from all claims, demands and causes of action arising from the failure of the indemnifying party to so comply, whether or not said indemnifying Party is named a party defendant to any action.

3.3 The Parties acknowledge that in entering into this Agreement and the Alliance created hereby, they are entering into a relationship which is difficult to define in all details prior to the commencement of activities hereunder. It is likely that situations will arise which have not been anticipated by the Parties and which may not be fully or adequately covered by this Agreement. In any such event, the Parties agree, in the spirit of mutual trust and cooperation which is stated throughout this Agreement, to each put forth its best efforts to address and resolve any such matters in keeping with the basic intent of the Alliance. Furthermore, the parties agree that this Agreement shall be amended as necessary.

IV: GOVERNING LAW/JURISDICTION

4.1 It is agreed that the proper venue for the resolution of any dispute arising hereunder, which is not settled in another manner, shall be the United States District Court of the Eastern District of Virginia, sitting in Fairfax County, Virginia.

4.2 The Parties agree that they shall attempt to resolve any disputes between them on an amicable basis, prior to the filing of litigious pleadings of any kind. All disputes, of any nature whatsoever, shall be handled by informal negotiation, in the first instance. In the event any such dispute is not resolved within sixty (60) days of the first notice of the dispute, the Parties agree to retain the services of a professional mediator to attempt to resolve the dispute, but the total time allotted to such mediation shall not consume more than thirty (30) days.

4.3 In the event mediation is not successful, either Party (or both Parties) may call for Arbitration to settle the dispute, by serving written notice to the other Party. Said Arbitration shall be binding and finally determinative of the dispute, unless both Parties agree for it to be non-binding.

V: WAIVERS/AMENDMENTS

5.1 No provision of this Agreement shall be, nor shall same be deemed to be, waived by either Party hereto unless the waiver is done in writing and signed by the Party to be charged.

5.2 No waiver of any provision in a given instance shall be deemed to be a continuing waiver, unless done in writing.

5.3 This Agreement may be amended only by a written amendment, executed by the authorized representatives of both Parties hereto.

5.4 Any written amendment, when executed, shall be attached to this Agreement and shall become a part hereof for all purposes.

5.5 Notwithstanding the foregoing, this Agreement as herein represented, constitutes the final and complete understanding as between the two parties regarding the Alliance at issue. No prior communications, letters, terms, agreements nor understandings shall be valid at and following the time that this Agreement is fully executed.

IN WITNESS WHEREOF, the Parties have caused this Alliance Agreement to be executed by their duly authorized representatives, in duplicate original counterparts, to be effective as of the date first shown above.

Party 1 a Virginia limited liability company
Party 2 a North Carolina limited liability company

By: _____
Name: _____
Title: _____

By: _____
Name: _____
Title: _____

EXHIBIT A

ALLIANCE AGREEMENT

SPECIFIC TERMS

BY AND BETWEEN

PARTY 1 (PARTY 1)

AND

PARTY 2 (PARTY 2)

TERMS: PARTY 1 and PARTY 2 hereby agree that for each Booking Event for which a performance contract shall be fully executed and performed, PARTY 1 will be due 5% of the Artist's or Athlete's Appearance Fee and PARTY 2 will be due 5% of the Artist's or Athlete's Appearance Fee–for a combined total of 10% being due to the Alliance and equally split between the Parties hereto.

PARTY 1 will facilitate the payment of the Appearance Fees for Booking Events that are performed or fulfilled by use of wire transfers, PayPal®, VISA®, MasterCard® and other forms of approved payment as further described in the Performance Agreement and Contract Rider to the Performance Agreement that shall govern all performances and appearances made at the Booking Events.

Prior to the payment of the Artists and Athletes that are booked for the Booking Event, the 10% fee described above shall be divided equally and appropriately allocated to PARTY 1 and PARTY 2 as above described. Following said distribution, the balance of the Appearance Fees shall be paid to the appropriate parties or party representatives of the Artists and the Athletes that are retained to make appearances or perform for Booking Events.

In the event that a Vendor/Owner of a venue or an Artist or Athlete fails to fulfill their obligations under a Performance Agreement, neither PARTY 1 nor PARTY 2 shall have any claim against each other; both Parties to the Alliance indemnify and hold each other harmless for any costs and damages that may result from a party's failure to perform under a Performance Agreement. Provided, however, that the Parties hereto shall have the right to seek costs and damages following from any breach committed by a Vendor/Owner or Artist or Athlete under a Performance Agreement.

Except as described in section 1.3 of the Alliance Agreement or for cause, the Alliance shall terminate automatically, without further notice, upon the final payment of all due fees and the resolution of any and all conflicts that may be waged against the Alliance following from the Booking Events scheduled to take place during the 100th CIAA Tournament® Event Weekend on March 2 and 3, 2012.

CHAPTER 9
WHAT ARE CAUSES OF ACTION AND REMEDIES FOR BREACH OF CONTRACT?

Rescission

The basis underlying the rescission of a contract is misrepresentation of some aspect of the contract. The person who learns there has been a misunderstanding of the contract has the choice to either affirm or rescind the contract. If both parties are reasonable, whatever the misunderstanding party requests can be amicably agreed to; however, on the other hand, the court can become involved to execute the rescission of the contract. Conversely, if the party that misunderstood the contract does not move swiftly enough to request a rescission, his indolence can render the contract legal and in force. Nevertheless, if conditions are not suspect, the objective of rescinding a contract is to place the parties to the contract back in the same position they were in before the contract was executed.

However, in the case of a fraudulent misrepresentation, the party that misunderstood the contract will not suffer due to his misunderstanding caused by the fraudulent misrepresentation; but the clock starts for him or her to move to rescind the contract as soon as he learns of the fraud. The court will consider when the fraudulent misrepresentation should have been discovered as it contemplates the case. Damages following from a guilty finding of fraudulent misrepresentation are only actual damages; the amount that the party who fell victim to the fraud actually lost.

Unconscionability

As discussed in the first chapter, briefly, unconscionability usually involves an unfair agreement in which one of the parties is in a superior bargaining position. The party in the inferior position usually stands to lose quite a bit at the result of the contract, and in the interest of the fairness, courts usually will act to bring fairness into the contractual affair.

The party that claims the contract is unconscionable will usually have to prove that there was a problem in the way the contract was formed (such as a lack of choice and negotiating power) and in the substance of the contract (such as tainted goods and usurious interest rates) itself. Courts can be flexible in how they handle these kinds of matters. They can either render the entire contract void due to unconscionability, or they can attempt to remedy the unconscionable portions of the contract and bring them to a state of fairness that will leave the contract intact, sans the courts modifications out of fairness. Damages are usually not awarded in these situations.

Frustration of Purpose

This problem usually arises when the subject of the contact is destroyed or when one of the parties to the contract dies. In the instance where the subject of the contract is destroyed, if the seller of the product or material bore the risk of loss (meaning, until the contract was executed and the deal was finished, the seller risked all damages and loss that might occur before such execution and conveyance of the property to the buyer), the court will usually still hold up the contract and the defense of non-performance will not save the seller from his or her responsibility under the contract. He or she will have to find an adequate substitute or pay the value of the property under the contract—his or her liability will not be excused.

On the other hand, if the buyer bore the risk of loss prior to the execution and finalization of the deal, because the property was not in the buyer's position during this time between entering into the contract and finalizing it, the court will dismiss the suit on the basis of frustration of purpose or impossibility.

Impossibility

Impossibility induces a court to excuse the non-performance of a party's duties under a contract in the situation where an assumption underlying the contract, or a pre-existing condition under the contract, renders performance of the contract impossible. For example, say you were in a car crash, where you arose unscathed, but your car was totaled. Before leaving home that day you had arranged for your teenaged neighbor to wash your car. Now that contract is an impossibility and no one will be at fault or liable.

Impracticability

This doctrine is very closely related to impossibility, however, whereas impossibility truly makes the performance of a contract impossible, impracticability occurs when an unexpected circumstance or burden occurs which makes it extremely hard, expensive or overly burdensome for one of the parties to comply with the contract. This is a subjective inquiry that will be performed by a judge if the parties cannot agree on the impracticability of a party's performance under the contract as planned.

Unclean Hands

The doctrine of unclean hands lies in equity. The doctrine is regularly stated as "those seeking equity must be acting in equity." The general idea is defendants usually bring this equitable defense to court with the complaint that the plaintiff has acted unethically or in bad faith in the performance of the contract. In other words, the plaintiff's hands are unclean. The defendant bears the burden of proving this to the court

Remedies in these matters usually do not come down to a dollar figure or damages. Usually courts order that the plaintiff rectifies the situation and specifically performs the contract as agreed upon or an injunction is put in place against the plaintiff acting in bad faith or unethically.

Note that, as the doctrine implies, a defendant's hands must also be clean when coming to court. A plaintiff has every right, offensively, to claim unclean hands against the defendant when an equitable ,affirmative defense or a request for equitable damages is targeted against it.

CHAPTER 10
GOING FORWARD, WHAT SHOULD YOU DO WHEN IT COMES TO CONTRACTS?

I cannot stress it enough; before you sign your name on any agreement or contract make sure you understand every provision, part, subpart, definition, nook and cranny of what you are signing off on. Make sure the contract reflects your understanding of the deal. If it does not, speak up and let the other side know, but don't you dare sign off on it. Never let anyone pressure you into signing an agreement that you don't really understand or totally agree with in all respects. I don't care how awkward it feels to sit in someone else's office and take your time to read, understand and ask questions about a contract before you agree to execute it with your signature. Be awkward in that moment; better to be awkward before executing a contract than to be downright uncomfortable in a court house when all falls down.

Contracts are wonderful tools to evidence plans of action and to get things moving. They propel intangible ideas and ideals into actions that manifest into reality. But make sure the reality your contract describes is the reality you really desire from the deal. If it's not right, it will bother you, so speak up. Miscommunications happen all the time, even when people are talking face-to-face. Remember, everyone is thinking from their own perspective in all instances, especially when it comes to deals and contracts.

Most times it is best to get objective third parties involved in the drafting and negotiation of the deal to ensure that all parties' expectations are accounted for in the final execution draft of the contract. Such objective third parties should be attorneys who are proficient in the field of understanding transactional/business law and who are very adept at drafting contracts. If you invest in an attorney's services before the deal is a go, you will be doing yourself a favor in the long run.

My clients who have given me the honor of not only drafting and negotiating their contracts for them and who have given me the privilege of helping them get their business started are clients that I delight in helping. Why? Because I have known their vision, their goals, dreams and expectations from the inception of their business and it brings me personal joy to see them grow. That makes drafting contracts and other documents for them that much easier, quicker and therefore cheaper. When you have someone on board with you from the start, who is an expert in helping people turn their dreams into reality, and who is willing to go to bat for you if hardcore negotiations have to take place to ensure that your desires are placed in writing in an effective contract, you will find yourself saving time, frustration and in the long run, worry lines and money.

Do not mistake the purpose of this book however. It is understood that a lot people turn to law in a box type of forms to start their businesses and execute agreements. It is also understood that in this economy money is tight. So this book has given you tips on what to look for, what to avoid, and how to handle yourself if you must go it alone without the help of legal counsel.

However, what is understood the most is this saying-because it never grows old and remains true: "You get what you pay for." A form cannot tell you what it is missing; a form cannot advocate for you; a form cannot negotiate new, novel ideas into itself that will reflect your goals and intentions with the clarity that will shut down any and all confusion from the other side. Attorneys are a good asset to invest in as you launch or manage your business endeavors. Contracts rule in this country. Let the ones who are experts at contracts rule how your transactions work out for your best benefit. Best of luck to you in all of your business endeavors.

ABOUT THE AUTHOR

Shaunè Hawkins Langston, Esq. has been an attorney for more than 10 years. She is a graduate of Northwestern University's School of Law ("Northwestern"), a top law school in this country and in the world. During her years at Northwestern she took several business courses at the Kellogg School of Management, one of the highest ranking business schools in the world as well. Her passion is business/transactional law and her specialization is in commercial real estate law. She was trained and has worked for three of the largest law firms in the world, including Hogan Lovells®, formerly known as Hogan & Hartson, LLP®, which is the law firm from which the Chief Justice of the United States Supreme Court, the Honorable John Roberts, last practiced private law before taking his seat as Chief Justice. When you learn from the best, you become the best and the best is what Mrs. Langston continuously strives to be and to achieve for her clients.

She is the owner of The Langston Law Firm,

PLLC; a business law firm based in Virginia, but she serves as general counsel for businesses in need of her services outside of Virginia as well. She is also a certified master life coach and the managing member of Let's Reign, LLC, a life coaching, business and legal consulting firm. She is active on Facebook, getting used to Twitter, LinkedIn and Pinterest and has started to blog at www.lavinepeake.blogspot.com (the name honors her ancestors). She enjoys her family, helping others, reading (romance novels in particular), writing, and her pit bull (Reign). As she says on her website for The Langston Law Firm, PLLC, her business is taking care of your business. If you are in need of legal counsel, think of The Langston Law Firm, PLLC–especially if it involves contracts (smile).

www.LangstonLawFirm.com
www.facebook.com/LangstonLawFirm
www.LetsReign.com

Copyright AND/OR Trademarks Acknowledgment Page

7-Eleven: Branded under the parent company Seven and I Holdings, Co, 7-Eleven is an international chain of retail convenience stores, which primarily operate as franchises.

Amazon Kindle: An E-reader, which has different models, that enables users to download several digital books via the Amazon Kindle store or even surf the internet (depenedent on the model of the Amazon Kindle.

CIAA: The Central Intercollegiate Athletic Association is a collegiate athletic conference consisting primarily of historically black colleges and universities who compete at the Division II level in the National Collegiate Athletic Association.

CIAA Tournament: An annual basketball tournament played by the colleges and universities who are part of the CIAA conference.

Fame: An American television series musical drama produced by Christopher Gore and consulting producer David De Silva, which aired in the 1980s.

Ferrari: Is an Italian sports car produced by Ferrari, S.p.A., which is a joint stock company based in Maranello.

Forrest Gump: Forrest Gump is a book copyrighted by Winston Groom, London: Black Swan, 1986. Forrest Gump is also a movie, based on the book, released in 1994, directed by Robert Zemeckis and starring Tom Hanks.

KDR program: The Amazon Kindle's Direct Publishing program that authors may opt-into to publish their works.

MasterCard: Also known as MasterCard Incorporated and MasterCard Worldwide, is an American multinational financial services corporation that principally facilitates the processing of payments between the banks of merchants and the card issuing banks or credit unions of the purchasers who use the MasterCard brand debit and credit card to make purchases.

PayPal: A global e-commerce business allowing payments and money transfers to be made through the Internet.

Phi Beta Kappa: The oldest honor society for the liberal arts and sciences with 280 chapters in the United States. It is widely considered to be the nation's most prestigious honor society.

Redbox: Redbox is a subsidiary of Outerwall, Inc. that specializes in the rental of DVDs, Blu-ray Discs, and video games via automated retail kiosks.

Visa: An American multinational financial services corporation that provides financial institutions with Visa-branded payment products that they can use to offer credit, debit, prepaid and cash access programs to consumers.

www.ingramcontent.com/pod-product-compliance
Lightning Source LLC
Chambersburg PA
CBHW051728170526
45167CB00002B/852